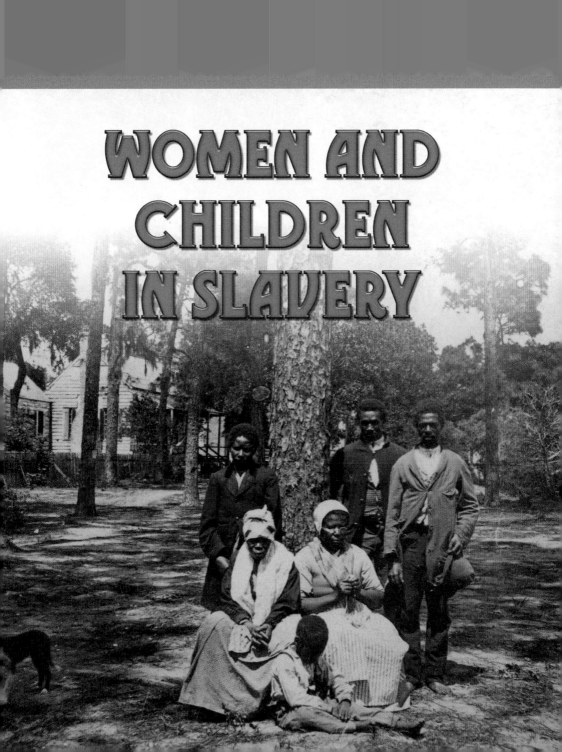

WOMEN AND CHILDREN IN SLAVERY

CAUSES OF THE CIVIL WAR

ESCAPE FROM SLAVERY: ABOLITIONISTS
AND THE UNDERGROUND RAILROAD

RECONSTRUCTION AND ITS AFTERMATH:
FREED SLAVES AFTER THE CIVIL WAR

SLAVE LIFE ON A SOUTHERN PLANTATION

SLAVE REVOLTS AND REBELLIONS

THE SLAVE TRADE IN COLONIAL AMERICA

WOMEN AND CHILDREN IN SLAVERY

WOMEN AND CHILDREN IN SLAVERY

CATHERINE A. GILDAE, PH.D.

MASON CREST

PHILADELPHIA | MIAMI

MASON CREST

450 Parkway Drive, Suite D, Broomall, Pennsylvania 19008
(866) MCP-BOOK (toll-free) • www.masoncrest.com

Printed and bound in the United States of America.

CPSIA Compliance Information: Batch #RGSL2019.
For further information, contact Mason Crest at 1-866-MCP-Book.

First printing
1 3 5 7 9 8 6 4 2

ISBN (hardback) 978-1-4222-4409-8
ISBN (series) 978-1-4222-4402-9
ISBN (ebook) 978-1-4222-7424-8

Library of Congress Cataloging-in-Publication Data
on file at the Library of Congress

Interior and cover design: Torque Advertising + Design
Production: Michelle Luke

Publisher's Note: Websites listed in this book were active at the time of publication. The publisher is not responsible for websites that have changed their address or discontinued operation since the date of publication. The publisher reviews and updates the websites each time the book is reprinted.

QR CODES AND LINKS TO THIRD-PARTY CONTENT

You may gain access to certain third-party content ("Third-Party Sites") by scanning and using the QR Codes that appear in this publication (the "QR Codes"). We do not operate or control in any respect any information, products, or services on such Third-Party Sites linked to by us via the QR Codes included in this publication, and we assume no responsibility for any materials you may access using the QR Codes. Your use of the QR Codes may be subject to terms, limitations, or restrictions set forth in the applicable terms of use or otherwise established by the owners of the Third-Party Sites. Our linking to such Third-Party Sites via the QR Codes does not imply an endorsement or sponsorship of such Third-Party Sites or the information, products, or services offered on or through the Third-Party Sites, nor does it imply an endorsement or sponsorship of this publication by the owners of such Third-Party Sites.

TABLE OF CONTENTS

KEY ICONS TO LOOK FOR:

Words to Understand: These words with their easy-to-understand definitions will increase the reader's understanding of the text while building vocabulary skills.

Sidebars: This boxed material within the main text allows readers to build knowledge, gain insights, explore possibilities, and broaden their perspectives by weaving together additional information to provide realistic and holistic perspectives.

Educational videos: Readers can view videos by scanning our QR codes, providing them with additional educational content to supplement the text. Examples include news coverage, moments in history, speeches, iconic sports moments, and much more!

Text-Dependent Questions: These questions send the reader back to the text for more careful attention to the evidence presented there.

Research Projects: Readers are pointed toward areas of further inquiry connected to each chapter. Suggestions are provided for projects that encourage deeper research and analysis.

Series Glossary of Key Terms: This back-of-the-book glossary contains terminology used throughout this series. Words found here increase the reader's ability to read and comprehend higher-level books and articles in this field.

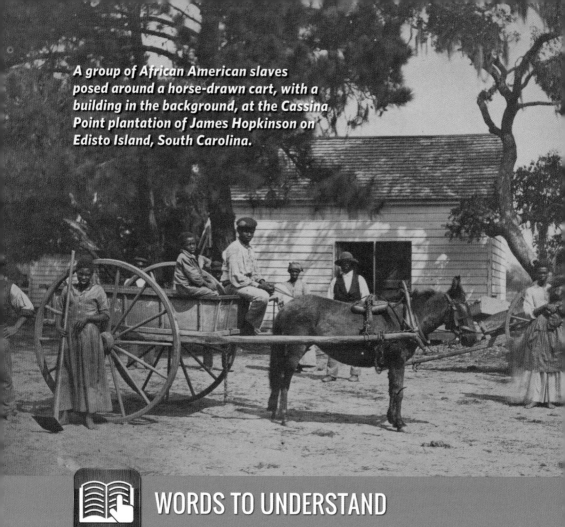

A group of African American slaves posed around a horse-drawn cart, with a building in the background, at the Cassina Point plantation of James Hopkinson on Edisto Island, South Carolina.

WORDS TO UNDERSTAND

codify—to create a system of rules or laws. In the context of slavery, it meant to create consistent laws about slaves and slavery.

gendered division of labor—tasks and job responsibilities are divided up based on whether it will be done by a male or a female. These divisions of labor along gender lines are based on custom and belief, but are far from universal from society to society.

infant mortality—the death of an young child in his or her first year of age.

CHAPTER 1

Women and Children in Slavery

Anta Majigeen Njaay was thirteen years old and a member of a wealthy family that lived in a village in western Africa when she was captured. In 1806 a group of warrior slaves arrived in her village on horseback. They killed many of the men, and took Anta and others, including some of her family members and slaves that her own family had owned, as prisoners. Her captors forced her and the others to march to the coast. After her arrival she was held in a prison, where she was eventually sold to European traders.

Then she began her journey across the Atlantic to the United States. The treacherous eight-week journey, known as the Middle Passage, claimed the lives of countless slaves between the shores of Africa and America. The slaves were kept below deck and packed in tightly. Disease spread rapidly in the cramped quarters and many died. Some slaves made their escape into the ocean; choosing death over enslavement. Despite the high death rate, slave traders made money from selling their human cargo in the Americas. Slaves who survived the two-month-long journey were sold at a significant profit.

The Africans sold as slaves came from different households, villages, and tribes. They spoke many languages, and had varied cultural traditions and religious beliefs. The practice of chattel slavery broke families apart. These people, sold as property, were forced to work in whatever capacity their owners saw fit.

WOMEN AND CHILDREN IN SLAVERY

In the early years most of the slaves brought to the colonies were male. Slave traders sought workers to fulfill the labor shortage and believed men would be best suited for doing such hard work. Interestingly, because of cultural differences, African villages were often more willing to part with men than with women. "In most West African societies women dominated agriculture," notes the book *Women's America: Refocusing the Past*. "Faced with the demands for captives, African villages preferred to surrender up their males and protect their female agriculturists; faced with a need for fieldworkers, Europeans preferred to purchase men."

Over time, the perceived value of male and female slaves shifted and changed. Slave owners realized that female slaves could help perpetuate the slave population. Female slaves became valuable because through reproduction, they produced new generations of slave workers. Colonial laws were amended to **codify** that the legal status of the mother would dictate the status of her child. A free woman's child would be free; a slave woman's child would be a slave.

Although male slaves greatly outnumbered women, there were female slaves from the start. The work that female slaves were assigned to do changed over time, also. In smaller farms

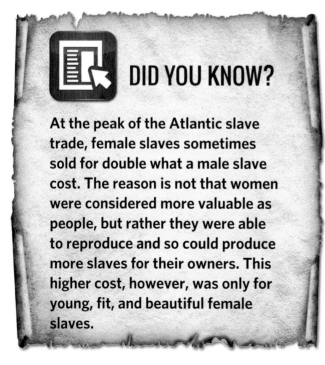

DID YOU KNOW?

At the peak of the Atlantic slave trade, female slaves sometimes sold for double what a male slave cost. The reason is not that women were considered more valuable as people, but rather they were able to reproduce and so could produce more slaves for their owners. This higher cost, however, was only for young, fit, and beautiful female slaves.

Sojourner Truth was a former slave who became a popular speaker in the 1840s. She sought the end of slavery and greater freedom for women in America.

and households, slaves of either sex often did the same sort of work. On larger plantations, slaves could specialize more, so there was more of a **gendered division of labor**, with women often doing household chores and men doing farm labor.

WOMEN'S WORK AND WORTH

In addition to their reproductive ability, female slaves were workers. Female slaves worked long hours and hard jobs, just like male slaves. As slavery grew and the number of slaves increased there was more gender-based division of labor. Female slaves worked the in the fields, in the trades, and in the home of their master. They cared for children—their own and their owner's— cooked and cleaned, sewed clothing for the family, and maintained fires in the home.

Women's role in society at the time of slavery helps to understand the role of women in slavery. Free women could not vote, own property, or train for most trades. Unlike slave women, however, free women were often viewed as delicate creatures to be protected. Slave women, were property, and were subject to all sorts of abuses. Masters physically beat or whipped their female slaves for failing to perform their duties. And they often raped

Photo from 1862 shows a nursery, where slave children were cared for, on Elliott's Plantation in Hilton Head, South Carolina. Slaves are seated in front of the building.

female slaves, or subjected them to other forms of sexual abuse. As *Women's America* notes, "The law did not protect enslaved women against rape or seduction." In fact, there were no laws prohibiting any type of abuse. The slave system was a more extreme version of the limited rights and protections that free women had in American society at the time.

Although female slaves performed the same work as male slaves, this was not due to any ideas about equality between the sexes. Female slaves performed the same work as men because their status was lower than that of free women or of enslaved men. Free women, particularly those with wealth or status, were generally protected from hard work. Slave women, because of their low status, were treated more like animals. In the later generations of slavery, especially as the international slave trade ended, some owners put protections for pregnant slaves and infants in place. However, such protections were more about protecting their property from harm, not about dignity or human rights for the women and children. Slave women also had little to no say over their children's lives, due to their legal status as property of the owner.

CHILDREN AT WORK AND AT PLAY

Childhood during the colonial era was very different from today; this is especially true for children born into slavery. **Infant mortality** rates were high, and many children died before they turned five years old. Those who survived infancy played and worked alongside their mothers until they could work independently.

There was no guarantee that even young children would remain with their parents, siblings, or extended kin. Once weaned, they could be sold or traded. Sojourner Truth, a woman who escaped from slavery and became famous as an abolitionist during the 1840s, once described the sale of slave children that she witnessed:

> There was snow on the ground, at the time of which we are speaking; and a large old-fashioned sleigh was seen to drive up to the door of the late Col. Ardinburgh. This event was noticed with childish pleasure by the unsuspicious boy; but when he was taken and put into the sleigh, and saw his little sister actually shut and locked into the sleigh-box, his eyes were at once opened to their intentions; and, like a frightened deer, he sprang from the sleigh, and running into the house, concealed himself under a bed. But this availed him little. He was reconvened to the sleigh, and separated for ever from those whom God had constituted his natural guardian and protectors, and who should have found him, in return, a stay and a staff to them in their declining years.

In addition to the risk of being sold, slave children learned what they saw growing up. By playing near their working parents in the home and in the fields, children learned how slaves were expected to behave. They also learned songs, games, and culture from their parents. Slave children took on adult working responsibilities much earlier than they do today, often around the age of eight or nine years old.

Slave owners recognized the value of having slave babies born, raised, and kept healthy, so they could become productive workers as adults. By the nineteenth century, it was fairly common on larger plantations for nurseries to be created for slave children. The female slaves would leave their infants and young children to be tended by older children, who would be watched in turn by older female slaves. Keeping children away from their working parents served two functions for the slave owners. With slave children at the nursery, their mothers did not need to take breaks to tend to their offspring and could therefore work longer and harder. The other purpose was to instill discipline in slave children from an early age. A result of having less contact with their parents was a more compliant, trained child.

Scan here for a brief overview of American slavery.

TEXT-DEPENDENT QUESTIONS

1. Why were female slaves considered uniquely valuable?
2. How was the legal status of a child determined under slavery?
3. In what ways were the rights of slave women and free women similar and different?

RESEARCH PROJECT

Listen to a narrative from the "Voices Remembering Slavery: Freed People Tell Their Stories" collection in the Library of Congress (https://www.loc.gov/collections/voices-remembering-slavery/about-this-collection/). Describe what you know about the person interviewed. How old were they when slavery ended or they became free? Compare and contrast the narrative you heard with that of another classmate. Write about how these narratives help us understand slavery better.

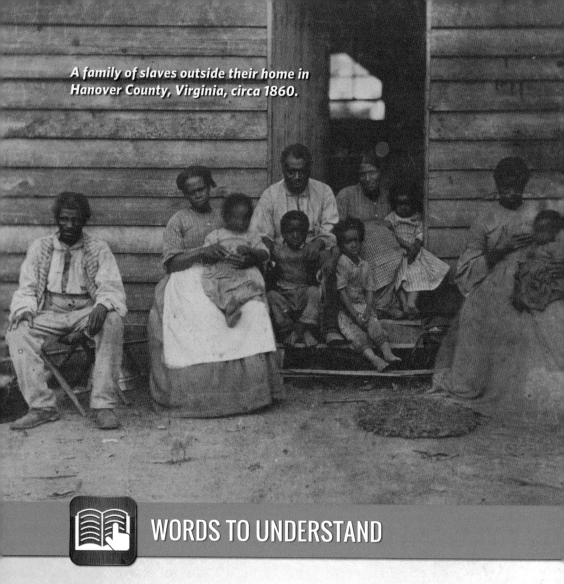

A family of slaves outside their home in Hanover County, Virginia, circa 1860.

WORDS TO UNDERSTAND

domestic—having to do with the care of the home. Domestic slaves were often assigned such tasks as cooking, cleaning, sewing, and caring for children or the sick.

mechanization—the use of machines to replace or assist manual laborers on a farm or in other industries.

heirs—people who inherit property, including money, after someone's death. Because slaves were considered property, ownership of slaves could be passed down through generations.

CHAPTER 2

Women in the House

Alice Green was born into slavery on a plantation in Alabama around 1860. Her father, Charles Green, worked in the fields, while her mother Milly worked as the cook in the "big house" where the white plantation owners lived. Alice was part of a large family: she had two older sisters, and would later have four younger siblings.

Because Milly Green worked in the house, she had the a close relationship with the white children in her care. Her daughter Alice described this relationship when she was interviewed during the late 1930s, as part of a federal government program to record and preserve the life stories of former slaves. "Mammy, she was the cook up at the big house, and when the white children came back from school in the afternoon, she would ask them to show her how to read a little book she carried around in her blouse all the time, and to tell her the other things they had learned in school that day," then 76-year-old Alice told an interviewer from the Federal Writers Project. "They [taught] her how to read and write."

Alice recalled the family treated her parents and the other slaves fairly well, although she also described a savage beating her father received for leaving the plantation without permission. After the Civil War ended in 1865, Alice reported that the white mistress of the plantation begged her slaves not to leave. The Green family continued living and working at the plantation for a year after the end of the war.

After being freed, Milly Green benefitted from being able to read. She was able to find work as a teacher and midwife. Alice would also grow up to work "cookin' for well-off white folks." Because she had grown up in the master's house, Alice understood the manners and customs expected by white families.

A DAY'S WORK FOR A HOUSE SLAVE

For most of the time that slavery was legal in the United States, a majority of enslaved people were **domestic** slaves. Most families owned small farms with just two or three slaves, not the plantation life so often seen in films such as *Gone With the Wind*. Slaves worked to keep the household running. Slaves did small scale farming and planting, as well as domestic chores such as cooking, cleaning, and laundry. On larger plantations, some female slaves were taught a specific trade, such as being a seamstress. In a smaller home, a domestic female slave would take responsibility for all of the necessary work.

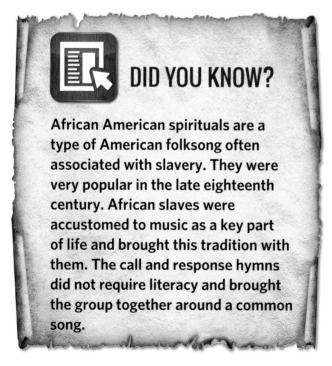

DID YOU KNOW?

African American spirituals are a type of American folksong often associated with slavery. They were very popular in the late eighteenth century. African slaves were accustomed to music as a key part of life and brought this tradition with them. The call and response hymns did not require literacy and brought the group together around a common song.

Cooking during the seventeenth, eighteenth, and most of the nineteenth century was very different from today. Pots and pans were made from heavy cast iron. It required skill and strength to lift and maneuver them into place. Cooking took place over an open wood fire, either in the fireplace or outside

Cooking was often done in large fireplaces like this one, using heavy cast-iron pots and pans.

Wash day on the plantation: children tend the fire under a cauldron of boiling water, while their mother scrubs clothes in a large wooden washtub.

in a dedicated kitchen space. The work was hot and dangerous. "Women ... risked scorching the hems of their petticoats or aprons," write historians Martha Katz-Hyman and Kym Rice in *World of a Slave: Encyclopedia of the Material Life of Slaves in the United States*. "Hot, heavy iron pots might easily tip, sending their scalding hot contents down the front of the cook's shins and across the feet." This risk was present whether they were cooking for the owner's family or for their own. Slave women often did both.

Slaves and their owners generally ate different meals. Slaves often cooked European-style dishes for the owner's family. Sometimes, slaves would be fed the leftover remains of these meals. In other cases, the plantation owner would provide slaves with a weekly ration of corn meal, meat, molasses, peas, greens, and flour. Some slaves, such as Alice Green's parents, were also allowed to cultivate their own gardens, fish, or trap small game such as possums, squirrels, and rabbits to supplement their weekly ration.

Doing the laundry also involved hard, manual labor. Slaves often had to make their soap by boiling animal fat with lye (potassium hydroxide). The process was hot and smelly, and exposure to the soap could result in painful chemical burns. The laundry process began with mending and repairing any damage to the clothes. Repairs included sewing on buttons or mending tears. After the repairs, the clothes were sent to soak in boiling hot water with the strong soap added. After the clothes had soaked for a day or more, slave women would remove them, hang them over a line, and beat them with sticks to help remove encrusted dirt and soap. As a final step, clothing was placed in boiled water again, then hung to dry on tree branches.

When then clothes were nearly dry, they were ironed. Unlike modern machines, the irons used by the slaves were heavy and heated by fire.

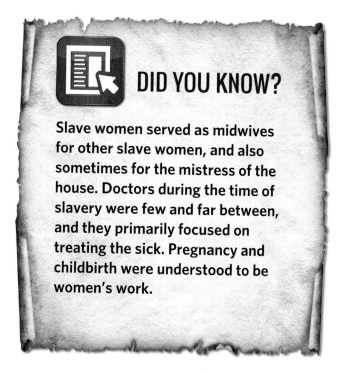

DID YOU KNOW?

Slave women served as midwives for other slave women, and also sometimes for the mistress of the house. Doctors during the time of slavery were few and far between, and they primarily focused on treating the sick. Pregnancy and childbirth were understood to be women's work.

During the 1770s, George Washington was one of many Americans who admired the poetry of Phillis Wheatley (1753-1784), a young black slave from Boston. This image of Wheatley appeared in her first book Poems on Subjects Religious and Moral, *published in London in 1773. When the book sold well, Wheatley was granted her freedom.*

The work was both delicate and dangerous, and the slaves risked receiving more burns in the process.

Thus, unlike today, doing laundry was a multi-day process. "Until **mechanization** and the introduction of crude washing machines began to offer some relief later in the nineteenth century," write Katz-Hyman and Rice, "washing clothes, bedding, and other fabrics was a difficult, labor-intensive, and arduous task that had to be performed regularly by women."

The work of female slaves was hard and potentially dangerous, and compounded by the risk of angering their masters. The consequences of not properly cooking the meals, cleaning the home, tending the children and the laundry, could include severe beatings or whippings.

Some historians have noted that there were trade-offs for domestic slaves. Domestic slaves often enjoyed more comforts than field slaves. They might be permitted to sleep in the attic of the big house, or have access to better food. However, they often were more closely watched than the field slaves. Domestic slaves

CHARMS, MEDICINE, AND HEALING

Many slaves were required to convert to Christianity by their masters. However, African religious practices still shaped slave customs and culture. Slaves believed that charms could be used as protection from evil spirits or to ward off illnesses. A charm could be almost anything—a button, animal parts, or a piece of ribbon. What gave these objects their power as a charm was the ritual carried out by a conjurer.

Female slaves hid charms meant for their protection under their skirts and dresses, and in their head wraps, so they would not be found by the Christian slaveowners. In addition, many slaves also employed household charms. These objects were hidden in their home or yard, and were thought to offer protection for the occupants.

When slaves became ill, they often sought out healers from their communities. Conjurers, both male and female, were believed to have power to communicate with the dead, administer botanical cures for ailments, terminate pregnancies, or cause harm others. The cures were generally a blend of folk medicine and faith, but some slave remedies included plants or substances that were unknown to white doctors.

The master's wife usually held the keys to storerooms and smokehouses, so that slaves could not enter them without permission.

had fewer opportunities for spend time with other slaves, or to earn some money of their own in the ways field slaves could do.

RELATIONSHIP WITH THE OWNER'S FAMILY

Household slaves had a relationship with the white owners' family that could be both intimate and quite distant. Women who worked in homes as domestic slaves came to know a great deal about the families they served. They drew baths for family members, cared for their children, and were privy to conversations. Some slave owners even took pride in describing how well they treated their domestic slaves, almost as if they were "part of the family." But there was an important distinction—domestic slaves could be sold at any time, and easily replaced by another slave.

Slave children often grew up alongside and played with the children of the family. When a slave was assigned to care for a child, it was common for that slave to stay with that child even as they grew up, married and left home. Upon the death of the master of the house, slaves were often divided among his **heirs**. These practices meant that domestic slaves often spent their entire lives with the same master and mistress.

DID YOU KNOW?

Female slaves often worked as seamstresses and made the family's clothes from cloth. Those who were talented were hired out to other families. This meant they had the opportunity to make money for themselves—possibly even enough to eventually buy their freedom.

In the South during the slave period, the house and surrounding buildings were usually considered to be under the direction of the plantation owner's wife or female relative. The mistress of the house kept a close watch on her domain. Valuables like sugar or silverware was locked away, and the mistress kept the keys. *World of a Slave* describes this division of physical space along gender lines:

> The master's house, together with outbuildings like the kitchen, smokehouse, icehouse, and dairy, and vegetable and flower gardens were predominantly female spaces.... Considering the master's house as a female space gives insight into how both slaveholding and enslaved women thought about, organized, and controlled their worlds. The mistress, or dominant slaveholding woman who was usually the wife or a relative of the male head of household, ran the house, issuing orders for clothing to be cleaned, mended, and made; for food preparation and storage; and for care and maintenance of valuable family goods like china, silver or silverplated ware, spices and liquor. An enslaved domestic servant, typically a woman, often served her mistress as a housekeeper."

Scan here to learn some of the ways slaves rebelled against their masters.

Mistresses could be cruel and they could be kind. It was her world to control and oversee. If the master—her husband—became sexually involved with a domestic slave, the mistress could demand that the domestic slave be sold. If anything went missing or was broken, the mistress could be exacting and cruel in handing out punishments. At the same time, some mistresses formed close relationships with their domestic slaves. Even though it was illegal in most Southern states to teach slaves how to read or write, numerous slave narratives recount tales of mistresses who helped their slaves achieve literacy.

TEXT-DEPENDENT QUESTIONS

1. How did slave women's household tasks under slavery differ from their modern equivalents today. Select one.

2. What were the relationships like between slave women and the mistress?

3. What is one of the ways slave women keep African traditions alive?

RESEARCH PROJECT

Read about the chores and household responsibilities in the eighteenth and nineteenth century, such as laundry or cooking. Consider especially the ways these jobs required strength and were dangerous. Write about how these jobs, so often associated with women, have changed in the twenty-first century and who does these types of jobs today.

Slave women often worked in the fields with men. These African Americans are picking cotton in Savannah, Georgia.

WORDS TO UNDERSTAND

autonomy—self-direction or self-governance. In the case of slaves, this meant not freedom but some ability to make life decisions for themselves.

bartering—a system of trade that involves discussing and offering one set of goods for another. For slaves this was a way to get better goods than they could make on their own, and to gain a sense of autonomy over their household labor.

kinship —a network or system of support. Traditionally kin is tied by blood and marriage, but in the case of slaves the term "fictive kin" is often used to describe the support system slaves provided for one another in the place of blood and marital bonds.

rooming house—a building with a number of private bedrooms, along with shared spaces for cooking, eating, and socializing.

CHAPTER 3

Women in the Fields

Emmaline Heard was only four or five years old when the Civil War ended and her family was freed from slavery. In a 1937 interview with the Federal Writers Project, Emmaline described her family's life before the Civil War, and the work her mother and other slaves performed on the plantation.

According to Emmaline, her father Lewis Heard had been sold to the Harper family in Georgia when he was eleven years old, and put to work in the fields operating a plow. Her mother, Caroline, also worked in the Harper family's fields for part of the time as a farm hand. She had other duties as well. "Every woman had a certain amount of weaving and spinning to do at home after coming in from the fields," Emmaline told the interviewer. "Until midnight, the spinning wheels could be heard humming in the slave cabins. At the hour of twelve, however, a bell was rung, which was the signal for the slaves to cease their spinning and go to bed." Caroline Heard also helped to prepare meals for the Harper family in the afternoon, and for her own family in the evening.

A DAY IN THE LIFE

Slavery in North America was tied to agriculture from the very start. At first, British colonists were focused on raising food to ensure their own survival, but as the colonies grew some colonists were able to expand their farms. They began to grow cash crops, such as

Scan here to learn about the importance of crops like tobacco.

tobacco and rice, that could be exported to Europe and sold at a profit. However, growing these crops required a larger labor force. African slaves were imported to solve the labor problem in the Southern colonies.

After about 1650, female slaves in the American colonies were regularly assigned to field labor. They tended crops alongside men. If they had infants, they did the work with the babies strapped to their backs. If they had young children, the children played nearby while their mothers worked. Once children were around eight years old, they joined in the work as well.

Working in the fields was especially hard, with long days spent planting, tending, and eventually harvesting the crops. It was long, hard work. The book *Women's America: Refocusing the Past* describes tobacco and corn farming:

> Organized into mixed-sex work gangs of anywhere from two to a rare dozen laborers, slave women and men worked six days a week and often into the night. Daylight work included planting, tending, and harvesting tobacco and corn by hand, without the use of draft animals. In the evening, male and female slaves stripped the harvested tobacco leaves from stems or shucked and shelled corn.

Those who worked in rice fields found a different rhythm to their days. Workers in rice fields needed to put in eight to ten hours to complete their daily tasks. Those who worked harder found themselves with some free time. Both rice and tobacco required a great deal of labor for the operation to be profitable. This meant that during peak times the master would hire additional slaves. It also meant slaves from other areas of the household were brought in to harvest. Slaves working long hours

Southern plantations needed large numbers of slaves to grow labor-intensive crops like tobacco, cotton, sugar, rice, and indigo (a plant from which a valuable blue dye could be made).

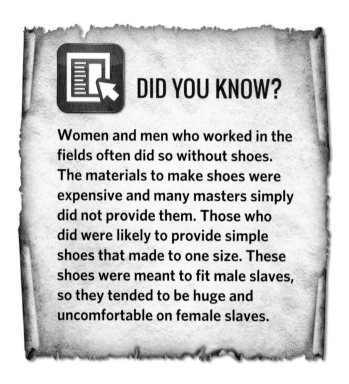

in the hot sun made their owners wealthy and shaped the course of American prosperity.

Most histories focus on plantation slavery. This model of farming, which was at its peak from 1793, with the invention of the cotton gin, until 1861, when slavery was abolished, is not the only form. Smaller family farms also relied heavily on slave labor for cheap labor. While it is not most of history, plantation farming is notable for its cruelty, long hours, and hard work. Cotton was a third key cash crop in the peak of slavery. It was more than a cash crop, it was necessary for clothing. Cotton was also brutal to harvest and done by hand for most of the time slavery was legal. The cotton gin increased the value of the crop and many plantations and larger farms expanded operations.

Slaves in the fields toiled long days, as did their counterparts in domestic work. Their lives and their days were not their own. Overseers on larger plantations kept the pace of work moving. Bells, horns, and other sounds signaled the start and end to the work. "Life for every young and adult enslaved individual revolved around work," explain Katz-Hyman and Rice in *World of a Slave*. "Work for slaves began when they were young children and continued into old age. Whether on a small farm or larger plantation, hard, unrelenting labor, day in and day out, was the fate of most field slaves." Through this labor and toil, slaves had one another to rely on for comfort, companionship, and **kinship**.

RELATIONSHIPS WITH OTHER SLAVES

Slavery on the plantation created interesting and unique connections. For plantations with a large enough plot of land there were slave quarters, separate from the house, though close enough to be watched by the master or his overseer. In the slave quarters, women who worked in the fields were able to make and maintain friendships with other women, with extended family, and with men. They were able to retain parts of their native cultures in Africa, either directly from their own lives or passed down to them from earlier generations. The slave quarters on larger plantations allowed slaves to enjoy some degree of privacy.

Slave quarters on a Louisiana plantation. Two multigenerational families would live in a cabin like this—one family on each side.

BARTERING FOR GOODS

Slaves did not own much and had limited power to earn money. This meant the likelihood of buying their freedom was very low. However, for some slaves—especially those who were skilled in a craft or trade—there were sometimes opportunities to earn money of their own. Enslaved women were sometimes able to grow crops, sew clothes, and raise a little livestock, such as chickens. They were able to trade what they grew or made with other slaves and also with whites in town markets. Often these trades were for other goods, but sometimes slave women could earn money, too. Markets provided more than a venue for sales, they also were social gatherings. While in the market, slaves could hear gossip and news, just as whites did.

Slaves who wanted to sell or trade goods in a town markets often started by setting up a wagon or makeshift stand. Over time, however, markets became more formal places. The wagons and stands were replaced by buildings. Some cities and towns began to require permits to sell goods. Some of these regulations and requirements were explicitly created to prevent slaves from selling their goods, especially for cash. Despite these restrictions, many slaves continued the practice of bartering and selling what they grew or made in their spare time. It was an important way for slaves to earn money, practice autonomy, and participate in the local economy.

In some areas, slaves lived in small communities of around fifty people but worked on different small farms or plantations. Because of availability of space, women and men shared living spaces. These spaces ranged from facilities similar to **rooming houses**, to living in basements or cabins where all slaves stayed together. Because of the numbers of people living in small spaces, disease spread quickly. These arrangements also meant little privacy from other slaves for a couple or family.

On plantations, especially during the peak of slavery in the nineteenth century, there were smaller, single-family houses or cabins for slaves. Some slave houses were divided down the middle with a private room on each side for a family. In such cases, women were able to run their domestic lives with some degree of privacy. They cooked and cleaned their own homes, raised their

Dormitory-style slave quarters on the Rockland plantation in Loudoun County, Virginia.

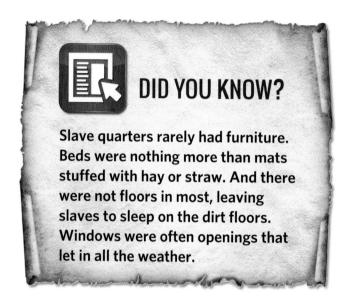

children, and included decorative personal touches. Many slave quarters contained secret storage spaces, often under the floorboards of the kitchen area. In these spaces a woman kept small charms or precious goods.

Slave housing dictated not only privacy and intimacy, but also a sense of belonging. Slaves, because of this sense of privacy, were able to tell stories and pass along cultural traditions. Slave women did what they could to keep their families fed, clothed, and sheltered with the resources they had available. They also formed bonds with other slaves. These bonds were necessary in a world where families were always under threat of separation.

Being a field worker meant that the work lasted from sunup to sundown. Women who worked in the fields all day tended to their families and homes after dark. They cooked and cleaned, cared for their children, and provided clothing for them. In other words, being a field slave did not alleviate their personal domestic duties. Often, female slaves worked together to care for children and to feed one another.

TEXT-DEPENDENT QUESTIONS

1. How were the cash crops different from one another?
2. When and how did slave women complete their domestic responsibilities?
3. How did slaves use what they had to achieve some degree of autonomy?

RESEARCH PROJECT

Learn about a market near you! Most major cities have some type of market, for example Faneuil Hall Marketplace in Boston (https://faneuilhallmarketplace. com/the-history-of-faneuil-hall/). Learn about a market near you and investigate its history. Does the market go back to slave times? What was sold there? Learn about not only the building but what existed before the building was built. Describe for your classmates what you've learned about the market, who used it, and what was sold there.

CASH!

All persons that have SLAVES to dispose of, will d
well by giving me a call, as I will give the

HIGHEST PRICE FOR

Men, Women, &
CHILDREN.

Any person that wishes to sell, will call at Hill's ta
vern, or at Shannon Hill for me, and any informa
tion they want will be promptly attended to.

Thomas Griggs.

Charlestown, May 7, 1835.

PRINTED AT THE FREE PRESS OFFICE, CHARLESTOWN.

Newspaper advertisement from 1835 for purchase of slaves—including women and children—by Thomas Griggs in Charlestown, South Carolina.

 WORDS TO UNDERSTAND

breeching—a rite of passage for enslaved boys, in which they were given their first pair of pants. It was considered a symbol of young adulthood.

pallet—a stuffed mat for sleeping upon. Usually filled with straw or hay for warmth and comfort.

material culture—physical aspects of culture, such as clothing or objects of importance and symbolism, such as the flag.

CHAPTER 4

Children at Work and Play

The lives of slave children were hard ones. From birth, slaves were property. They were commodities that could be bought, sold, and traded for the profit of another person. They played games and sang songs, but the conditions were brutal. By today's standards, they had no childhood whatsoever. There was no opportunity for education unless a kind master or white child took it upon themselves to teach the child. Those who survived to adulthood had a hard life ahead of them.

Tempie Cummins was one of millions of people born into slavery in America. She was born in Brookeland, Texas, but didn't know her date of birth or the specifics. Her parents, Jim and Charlotte Cummins, were both from Alabama, and she had a brother and four sisters.

In an interview with the Federal Writers Project during the 1930s, Tempie described her life as a slave before the Civil War. She recalled being sold to a new household around the time that she was eight years old. Her owners provided her with clothes and a **pallet** for sleeping. The clothes were usually cast-offs from the white children, but she recalled a "home-spun" dress given to her one Christmas. That was the dress she was expected to wear any time company came over. The rest of the time she wore the cast-off clothes, pinning them around her body because they were too big. She wore the same clothes until they were "strings."

Former slave Tempie Cummins, photographed in Texas in 1936.

Tempie described how the white children tried to teach her to read and to write. But, she was always working and did not learn much. The household had thirty or forty acres and raised cotton, corn, and potatoes. They worked all daylight hours, and Tempie recalled that the master would punish anyone who did not work hard enough. Her mother worked in the home as a cook and would routinely listen to the family's conversations.

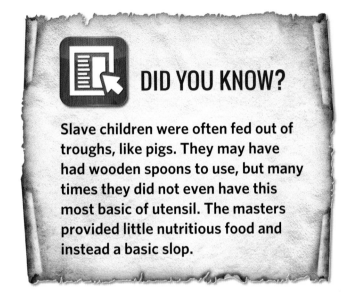

DID YOU KNOW?

Slave children were often fed out of troughs, like pigs. They may have had wooden spoons to use, but many times they did not even have this most basic of utensil. The masters provided little nutritious food and instead a basic slop.

It was by listening that her mother learned of emancipation. Charlotte overheard the master saying he would not tell his slaves that freedom had come. She ran to the fields and told the others that they were free. The master was angered by her actions and chased after them with his gun. Charlotte managed to hide in the ravine and had others bring Tempie to her so both escaped to freedom against their master's wishes.

INFANCY AND EARLY CHILDHOOD

In the seventeenth and eighteenth centuries, diseases and lack of proper nutrition meant that infants had a high mortality rate. This was especially true of infants born to slave mothers. Those who survived infancy had to battle with childhood illnesses, too. The risks were greater for slave children because of their living conditions. Slave masters were unlikely to seek out a doctor's care for adult slaves, and even less so for children.

In the late eighteenth century and the nineteenth century, changes began to occur. One of these was the rise in plantation-style farming, which required larger groups of slaves, in the South. Another other key shift was an increase in the gendered division of labor. Women still worked in the fields, but increasingly their children were left in the care of others while they did so.

What these changes meant in practice was that women in society were expected to be more focused on the home and on the care of children. For slaves, these changes meant leaving their infants and young children in the care of others. Older female slaves and younger female slaves, children by today's standards, were often assigned child caring roles. The infants of slaves were kept in the nursery and tended to by other slaves so they could work in the fields or other jobs around the house. This system enabled socialization from birth and also got women back to work quickly after giving birth.

Slave children often played with the white children of the household. While in some places there were prohibitions on

Kids in the 18th Century

Scan here to learn more about life for children in the eighteenth century.

mixed play, for the most part the children of the household played together. Though they played together, there were disparities in toys and resources. White infants had carriages and prams, cradles, and other ways to comfort and care for baby. Slave infants were set down on mats and swaddled in cloth scraps. White children had dolls and dollhouses, books, and other toys. Slave children had homemade dolls and few toys. These differences in infancy and childhood mirrored and reinforced the differences that would last their lifetimes.

TRANSITION TO ADULTHOOD

Their time in the nursery was brief, however. Slave children were able to work from the time they were six or seven years old. They learned from a very early age how to do the jobs of their parents, older children and other slaves. By the time a child was old enough to work there was additional risk of being sold. Able-bodied children were assets that owners could sell or trade as they saw fit, and often did. Children worked in the fields, and also in the home cleaning, cooking, preparing laundry, and trained under their parents as seamstresses and other trades.

Clothing is an interesting piece of **material culture** that denotes the transitions from infancy to childhood and on to adulthood. Master's were responsible for providing clothes to their slaves and often did so on a schedule. This often meant new clothes for slaves twice per year, once in summer and once in winter. Children were not routinely provided with clothing. The clothing was provided so that slaves could work. As a result, the parents made use of what they had to make their children clothing. Clothes were also passed down from one child to the next.

All infants until the modern era tended to be dressed alike in unisex gowns. These garments were handed down from one infant to the next and were designed for quick diaper changes. As a child grew older, the unisex garment evolved into something akin to a

CHILDHOOD AFTER SLAVERY ENDED

Clarissa Scales was born into slavery on a plantation in Plum Creek, Texas, in the late 1850s. As a slave she was responsible for tending the fires and caring for hogs in Plum Creek, Texas. Slavery ended during her childhood, but her parents stayed on the plantation and rented farmland after emancipation. This was not an unusual arrangement, because the plantation and farm owners still needed help, and slaves often did not have the resources necessary to set out on their own. Now, instead of being slaves, they were workers on the farms and plantations.

After emancipation, freed slaves had access to education. Clarissa had an opportunity to attend school. In her narrative, Clarissa recalled that members of the Ku Klux Klan came to the school she attended. They tried to intimidate her teacher and make him stop teaching the black children. The teacher was scared, but finished the school year. The following year the school hired another teacher.

Clarissa wanted to be a teacher herself one day, but her father discouraged this ambition. He told her that learning to read and write was enough. So Clarissa gave up this dream and worked on the family farm. She got married when she was fifteen years old, and eventually had five children. She and her husband also had a small farm, about nineteen acres.

When Clarissa was interviewed by the Federal Writers Project in 1937, she was a widow. The photo of her on this page was taken at that time. She was proud that each of her children had more education and opportunities than she had received.

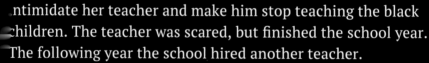

short dress for both male and female children. **Breeching** for boys was considered a rite of passage and marker of adulthood. Female children, too, got clothes akin to those of adult females, often a longer dress or a skirt and top, as a sign of adulthood. Once the owner gave the child proper clothing it was a sign of the start of their work life.

EDUCATION

In most of the states with slavery, it was illegal to educate a slave. Children, therefore, grew up working and not learning to read, write, or do math. While literacy was illegal for most slaves, it did not mean they learned nothing. Quite the opposite, as slave narratives discuss, children learned spiritual hymns, stories, and legends from the elders, and how to engage in the trades of their owners.

Though rare, slave children sometimes learned to read and write. If their parents, especially mothers, were literate they passed on their knowledge to their children. As was the case with Tempie Cummins, sometimes the white children of the household also attempted to teach slave children to read and write. And on very rare occasions, the mistress or master would educate their slaves.

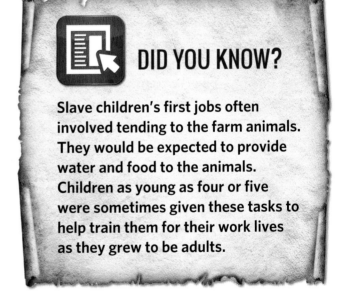

DID YOU KNOW?

Slave children's first jobs often involved tending to the farm animals. They would be expected to provide water and food to the animals. Children as young as four or five were sometimes given these tasks to help train them for their work lives as they grew to be adults.

Much of the education that slave children had access to was in the form of training for work. They learned trades and farming methods, to cook and mend clothing. Even the games were often related to learning about slavery and their role in the household or society.

GAMES SLAVE CHILDREN PLAYED

Like their white counterparts, slave children played games. Among the famous games is Hide the Switch. In this game the children would find a small branch and hide it for others. Once found, the child who found it would chase the others around. If caught, the child would receive lashes with the switch from the child who found it. This game reinforced lessons of slavery.

Another game children played was akin to volleyball or dodgeball, called Haley Over or Anti-Over. The children divided into two groups and threw a ball over a building. When the child on the other side caught it, they ran around to try and hit the kids on the other side. Clapping games like children still play today were also very popular. Hand claps like Miss Mary Mack were a way for slave children to pass their time in the fields. By some accounts, African games like mancala were common and had the added benefit of teaching slave children to reliably count.

Some children were fortunate enough to play more traditional children's games like skipping rope or walking on stilts. Slave children also sang and danced, engaged in dramatic play, and reenacted life on the plantation.

In addition to formal games, slave children enjoyed spending time outside exploring nature. Some slave children experienced a great deal of freedom so long as they stayed out of the way. With their time they chased rabbits, explored the forests and streams, and even hunted or fished to help provide food for their families.

TEXT-DEPENDENT QUESTIONS

1. How did child-caring change over time for slaves?
2. What sorts of things did children do to play during slavery?
3. When did a slave leave childhood and enter into adulthood?

RESEARCH PROJECT

Choose one of the primary sources from http://chnm.gmu.edu/cyh/case-studies/141?section=introduction and explore what it was like to be a slave child. The introduction provides context. Write an essay about how the what you discovered can better help us understand how children experienced slavery.

Rough furnishings, including a rope bed and a wooden cradle, in slave quarters at Boone Hall Plantation, near Charleston, South Carolina.

WORDS TO UNDERSTAND

fictive kin—people who are not related by blood or marriage, but have a strong emotional bond that is similar to a family relationship.

infanticide—the crime of killing a child younger than one year of age.

informal marriage—a relationship in which two people consider themselves married, although their union is not recognized by civil or religious authorities.

miscegenation laws—legislation passed in the Southern states that made it illegal for blacks to marry whites. Some of these laws predated the Civil War and were never repealed after the war ended.

CHAPTER 5

Marriage and Kinship Ties

"I never knowed my own pa, 'cause he 'long to 'nother man and was sold away 'fore I's old 'nough to know him," a former slave named Hannah Scott told a Federal Writers Program interviewer during the late 1930s. "Dey didn't have no marriage back den like now. Dey just puts black folks together in de sight of man and not in de sight of Gawd, and dey puts dem asunder, too."

Hannah's Scott's history was not unusual for slaves. While many owners, including her parent's owner, allowed slaves to form relationships— what Harvard historian Nancy Cott calls **informal marriage**—the slaves were not considered to be legally married by secular courts or religious authorities. While fellow slaves often respected these informal marriages, as Hannah notes they were often not acknowledged as legitimate by slaveowners. Slaves were property that could be bought and sold without respect to marriage or family bonds.

In her narrative, Hannah Scott says that her childhood master owned a small farm and about nine slaves. At some point he had to sell Hannah and her mother, probably to pay debts. Hannah recalled that the master and his wife cried when she and her mother were sold. But he sold them, nonetheless, and the Scotts moved to Arkansas.

Their new owner had a much larger operation, including over a hundred slaves and an overseer. Hannah grew up on this new

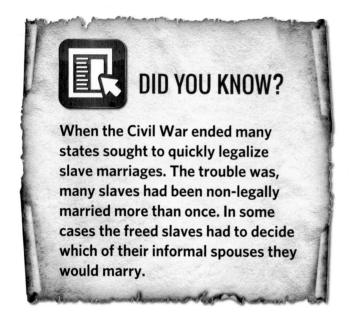

DID YOU KNOW?

When the Civil War ended many states sought to quickly legalize slave marriages. The trouble was, many slaves had been non-legally married more than once. In some cases the freed slaves had to decide which of their informal spouses they would marry.

plantation and was put to work in the fields as soon as she was old enough. They worked from sunup until sundown, and the new master beat or whipped them regularly. The exception to non-stop work was Sunday, when the slaves were given time to do their own wash and mend their own clothes.

Once a month a white preacher would come to town and preach a message of obedience to the master.

Her former master, whom Hannah referred to in her interview as "my White Pa," tried to buy Hannah, her mother, and their children back. However, their new owner refused to sell, and even threatened to kill Hannah's mother if she tried to run away.

After the slaves were freed at the end of the Civil War, the Scott family remained on the large Arkansas plantation and worked the land for pay. Unlike her parents, when Hannah became an adult she had the opportunity to become legally married. She and her husband, a railroad worker, had five children together. At the time she told her story, Hannah was living with her grandson.

THE MEANING OF MARRIAGE

Marriage, while long thought of as a religious institution, is also a legal and social one. There are many ways to be married, and in contemporary society these three aspects are often blended. However, during slavery, the legal aspects of marriage were out of reach. Slaves were not only the property of someone else, but the laws in Southern states prohibited legal marriage for most black Americans—not only between slaves, but even between free blacks and whites in some states.

Owners could be benevolent and allow their slaves to engage in an informal marriage. The social tie of marriage was beneficial to both slaves and their owners. Marriage was a bond between man and woman at the time, and considered the foundation of the family. A married couple was expected to have children. It was because of this connection between marriage and children that owners encouraged their slaves to informally marry. Allowing slaves to have families also encouraged stability among the black communities of the South. When slaves were responsible for the safety of their children and spouses, it became harder for them to overtly rebel against their white masters.

Because of the nature of slavery, black women were not always able to freely choose their husbands. Some masters only allowed their female slaves to marry male slaves that they owned. This way their female slaves would not have to leave the plantation to live with their husbands. Also, the children of female slaves became the property of the owner. A slaveowner who allowed his male

Scan here to learn more about how families looked out for each other.

In slave communities, a man and woman that wished to marry would jump over a broom in front of witnesses. This was a signal to the community that they were committed to an exclusive relationship.

slave to marry another owner's female slave gained nothing from this arrangement, and so was less likely to permit such a bond.

The religious aspects of marriage are also important to consider. Most slaves were raised as Christians, and required to attended the church of their white household. Whites and slaves would not sit together—and sometimes did not even attend the same service—but many slaves attended the white church. White preachers were not willing to marry slaves in the church. This helped to protect white slaveowners—if slaves were married in the Christian tradition, an owner could be accused by church leaders of interfering with the couple's sacred vows if he sold members of the slave family. By keeping slave marriages informal, the master could—and did—manage his property as he saw fit, and primarily for his own benefit.

In many cases, slaves created their own ceremonies of recognition for marriages. The expression "jumping the broom" is an example of a slave tradition marking the official start of a marriage. In this tradition the couple would exchange vows before other slaves. There was an officiant to oversee the exchange. As the ceremony drew to a close, brooms were laid down in front of the couple. Together, as a symbol of their unity, the couple jumped across the broomsticks and into their marriage. These informal marriages were outside of legal or religious regulation but were upheld and respected by other slaves.

THE IMPORTANCE OF KINSHIP

Due to the nature of slavery, the family bonds of informal marriages could be temporary. Thus in slave communities, extended families—including aunts and uncles, grandparents, and cousins—made up an extensive network of support and love. This

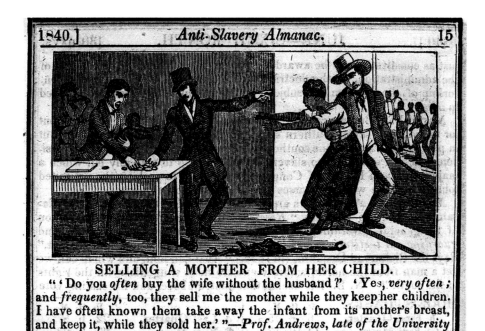

An illustration from the Anti-Slavery Almanac of 1840 shows a slave woman being sold and separated from her young child.

extended family provided moral guidance and support, financial support. They celebrated together at holidays and weddings, and mourned together at funerals and in hard times.

Slave communities also placed great importance on what modern anthrolopologists refer to as **fictive kin**. Unrelated slaves often formed kinship bonds, protecting and teaching each other like family members would. These bonds could be formed and re-formed over time as slaves were sold and traded away, and replaced by others. Kinship bonds did not replace the familial bonds marriage and bloodline, but they did provide a strong social network of support and care.

DID YOU KNOW?

Slave girls and boys often engaged in different types of games. They were influenced by the gender roles of their time. Girls tended to play games that encouraged keeping house and dances or parties. They also had less freedom to explore like the male slaves did.

Because of the sale of slaves, some women entered into more than one informal marriage, and had children by different fathers. They always knew their children could be removed and sold with no notice. Slave auctions drew buyers from out of state, and once sold family members would be separated permanently.

In addition, female slaves were subjected to sexual abuse and rape by their white owners. This abuse started early—often in adolescence—and could last a lifetime. Despite these horrible circumstances, these women loved and cared for the children who resulted from these acts.

Slave narratives are filled with stories of hope and love involving families. Slave women made great sacrifices to be

THE LEGACY OF SLAVE MARRIAGE LAWS

Laws prohibiting or regulating marriages involving black Americans did not disappear after slavery ended. Laws that prohibited anyone who was not white from marrying someone who was white, remained in several Southern states well into the twentieth century. It was not until 1967, when the US Supreme Court struck down the remaining miscegenation laws as unconstitutional, that this legacy of slave marriage laws finally disappeared.

The word "miscegenation" is derived from the Latin words *miscere* ("to mix") and *genus* ("race"). Miscegenation laws regulated the marital and sexual relationships that adults could have with people of other races. There were laws prohibiting slaves from marrying one another, but also from marrying free blacks or members of other races. There were also laws banning mixed-race couples from having children together. It was a considered a felony, or serious crime, to break the law, and punishment could include physical beatings or prison time.

The beliefs behind these laws were based on racist ideas about heritable traits. The fear was the in "mixing" the blood of the different races the ideal traits of the so-called superior race would be lost. This belief, in large part, was why the greatest restrictions were against a white person marrying someone who was not white. Several states permitted people who were not white to marry other non-white people. This idea of preserving "racial integrity" was not based on science, but rather on fear. Today geneticists study racial variation and have evidence to show that nearly everything about humans is identical at the genetic level, and there are no genetic markers for what society calls race. Genetics have demonstrated that most variation takes place within given racial groups, not between diffrent racial groups.

Thomas Jefferson, a Founding Father and third president of the United States, had a longtime relationship with female slave Sally Hemings. She bore at least six children that Jefferson fathered. Her children were also slaves, until Jefferson freed them at the end of his life. Hemings herself was never officially freed, and no portraits of her exist.

with their children, and to shield them from harm, and children sometimes overcame obstacles to be reunited with their mothers, too. Family life as a slave was filled with challenges of bravery and love.

MOTHERS AND CHILDREN

Among the earliest generations of African slaves brought to North America, there were far fewer women than men. As a result, there were not many slave children in those first decades. In fact, the slave population remained relatively stable through the seventeenth and early eighteenth century.

Over time, the system of slavery evolved and lawmakers created laws about slave offspring. These laws made the offspring of a slave woman also a slave. In time the numbers of children born into slavery rose. Some scholars have even argued that these laws encouraged masters to seduce or rape their female slaves to create more slaves.

It is not universal, however, that slave owners wanted their female slaves to reproduce. Slave owners who held only a few slaves did not usually permit their female slaves to have children. An infant represented another member of the household—one that had to be fed, clothed, and cared for, and could not work for many years. As a result, female slaves were sometimes sold if they became pregnant, or both mother and baby were sold shortly after birth.

A former slave named Jake Terriell, who lived in Texas, described the all-too-common scene when slaves were sold in 1937. "I seed slaves sold and you has heared cattle bawl when de calves took from de mammy and dat de way de slaves bawls," he explained to a Federal Writers Project interviewer.

THE PARTING "Buy us too."

There are countless narratives where former slaves told tales of children being sold away or mothers taken from their families. Sometimes it was fathers

This abolitionist card from the 1850s depicts the terrible impact of slavery on families. A woman, holding her child, begs to accompany her husband who has been "sold South."

who took their children, such as the case of J.W. Terrill of DeSoto Parish, Louisiana. "My father took me away from my mother when at the age of six weeks old and gave me to my grandmother, who was real old at the time," he recalled. "Jus' befo' she died she gave me back to my father, who was my mammy's master." In other words, Terrill's father was a white slaveowner, who sold his mother and gave the infant to his enslaved grandmother to raise. Some historians have estimated that approximately one-third of all enslaved children were separated from their parents due to the sale of one or more of the family members.

ESCAPING BY ANY MEANS NECESSARY

Margaret Garner was a slave woman who ran away with her husband, Robert, and several other families in 1856. They managed to reach Cincinnati, Ohio, but were surrounded by slave catchers before they could go further North. The Fugitive Slave Act of 1850 required authorities to help return escaped slaves to the South. Margaret killed her two-year-old daughter rather than seeing her returned to slavery. She was prepared to kill her other children, and herself, but was captured before she could complete this task.

Most slaves did not try to kill their children after they were born, but some did try to terminate their pregnancies. The conjurers of slave communities were rumored to possess charms and potions that could lead to spontaneous abortion. This was more common if the pregnancy was a result of relations with the master.

Slave women often felt compelled to stay on the plantation and care for their children, rather than trying to run away. Slave owners recognized and exploited this dilemma to keep their slaves in place. Those slaves who had families, they believed, were less likely to run away.

After the Civil War ended, some freed slaves took out advertisement in hopes of reconnecting with loved ones. For example, an ad was placed in the *Colored Tennessean* newspaper shortly after the war ended. It read, "Information wanted. Information is wanted of my mother, who I left in Fauquier country, Va. In 1844, and I was sold in Richmond, Va. To Saml. Copeland." Ads like this, or the one pictured at right from the *Dallas Express*, offer a testament to the bonds between women and their children, and the desire for reunification even years later.

> **Want to Know**—of the whereabouts of my daughter, Mrs. Victory Williams, last heard of she was in Regin, Texas, any information concerning her will be highly appreciated, address Mrs. Lina Williams, 117 West First street, St. Angelo, Texas.
> 5-3-1t

TEXT-DEPENDENT QUESTIONS

1. What are the different types or practices of marriage? Which of these was available to slaves?

2. Why did some masters encourage their slaves to marry?

3. In what ways did slaves compensate or make up for their lack of legal rights to form meaningful relationships including by marriage?

 RESEARCH PROJECT

Using your school library or the internet, find out more about Mildred and Richard Loving, the couple behind a landmark 1967 Supreme Court case that ended interracial marriage bans in the United States. Write a one-page paper about what you would do if you could not marry the person of your choice because of the laws at the time. Share your paper with the class.

This small log cabin housed a slave family on a Maryland farm during the 1800s.

abolitionist—someone who worked to end slavery. Often these women and men formed groups, attended lectures, and read papers to inform themselves, and raised money to help slaves escape.

micro-aggressions—intentional or unintentional insults or treatment meant to send a negative message to the targeted person.

manumission—the act of an owner formally freeing his or her slaves.

CHAPTER 6

Female Slaves and Resistance

Harriet Jacobs was born into slavery in 1813 in Edenton, North Carolina. She lived with her family until the age of six, when her mother died. She was then taken from her family and became the property of Margaret Horniblow, her mother's mistress. Horniblow was a most unusual mistress in that she taught her young slave girl to read and write! Harriet Jacobs spent the next six years with Horniblow, until her death.

In her will Margarget Horniblow passed ownership of Harriet Jacobs to her niece, Matilda, who was only three years old at the time. Because of Matilda's youth, her father Dr. James Norcom essentially became Harriet's new owner. Though Harriet was only twelve years old at the time, she had to fight off the sexual advances of her new master for almost a decade. Eventually, the abuse became so unbearable that she had to escape. She ran away from the plantation in 1835, and hid from her master for seven years. She later described her hiding spot, in the attic of her grandmother's cabin in a nearby swamp, in her memoir:

> It was a pent roof, covered with nothing but shingles, according to the southern custom for such buildings. The garret was only nine feet long, and seven wide. The highest part was three feet high, and sloped down abruptly to the loose board floor. There was no admission for either light or air.

She hid in this small space for all those years with the help of her family, and kept her spirits up by hearing the sounds of her children. Eventually, she escaped to the north in 1842, and wrote a narrative of her life as a slave during the 1850s. Jacobs's tale seems unbelievable today, but the facts were verified by historians during the 1970s and 1980s.

DAILY RESISTANCE

Escaping to the North, as Jacobs did, was the ideal way for individual slaves to resist the unfair system, but it was also dangerous. Slave owners would hire men to track and capture runaways. Another type of resistance to slavery was rebellion on a larger scale, which occurred when slaves would fight back against their masters. Among the more notable revolts of American history were two that occurred in Virginia: one led by a slave named Gabriel in 1800, and another led by Nat Turner in 1831. However, slave revolts were often put down by white authorities, and those who took part in them were killed or mutilated. Therefore, for most slaves, the most common form of resistance

To learn how the Fugitive Slave Act of 1850 made it harder for slaves to escape, scan here.

HORRID MASSACRE IN VIRGINIA·

The Scenes which the above Plate is designed to represent are—Fig. 1, a Mother intreating for the lives of her children.—2. Mr. Travis, cruelly murdered by his own Slaves.—3. Mr. Barrow, who bravely defended himself until his wife escaped.—4. A comp. of mounted Dragoons in pursuit of the Blacks.

A Virginia newspaper illustration from 1831 shows scenes from Nat Turner's rebellion. The slaves killed more than 50 people before state authorities could regain control.

occurred in the form of daily actions that pushed back against the master and mistress.

Many slave narratives point to smaller forms of daily resistance, or **micro-aggressions**. Slaves would describe feigning illness, destroying crops, avoiding work, and even poisoning their owners as ways that they fought back against the plantation system. These small forms of resistance were difficult to trace to a single slave, but they still made an impact on the economic activity of the plantation. Female slaves were often assigned jobs close to the family, and therefore had the best opportunities for such actions. Additionally, these forms of resistance were

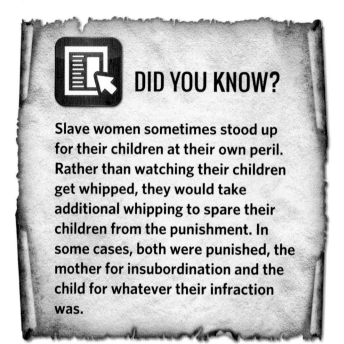

available to women even if they had child-caring responsibilities or were limited by pregnancy. "Slave women wove resistance into the fabric of daily life under slavery," explains Indiana University historian Amrita Chakrabarti Myers.

Women had additional sources for resistance because of their ability to reproduce. These female forms of resistance offered women the chance to push back against masters who were often cruel and used them sexually. Female slaves used what they had available to them to fight back. Myers found examples of slave women effectively using contraception to keep themselves from getting pregnant by white masters, who wished to add their mixed-race children to the slave population. In her review of slave narratives, Myers also found mention of "two instances of infanticide, twelve cases of resisting rape, and four cases of women who resisted marriage."

RUNAWAYS AND THE UNDERGROUND RAILROAD

Certainly, many women sought freedom and risked their lives to escape like Harriet Jacobs did. Many utilized the Underground Railroad, a network of secret routes that escaped slaves could follow to reach the free states of the North or Canada, where slavery was illegal. Abolitionists established and maintained safe houses and hiding places along the way. At its peak in the

Harriett Tubman, one of the most famous members of the Underground Railroad, is said to have made nineteen trips back into the south, freeing over 300 slaves. She risked her life each time because the Fugitive Slave Act of 1950 increased the penalties for anyone found helping runaway slaves.

mid-1850s, thousands of slaves reached freedom through the Underground Railroad each year. About 20 percent of the slaves who escaped through the Underground Railroad were women.

Sometimes, escaped slaves went back to the South to guide others along the Underground Railroad. Harriet Tubman is the most famous of these "conductors." She ran away from a plantation in Maryland in 1849, but returned nineteen times over the next eleven years, risking her life to bring more than 300 slaves to freedom.

Ellen Craft was another woman who escaped slavery and went on to help others. She was a mixed-race slave, but could pass as white. To escape, she dressed like a white slaveholder, pretending that she could not write due to injuries. She traveled with her husband William, who was disguised as her personal

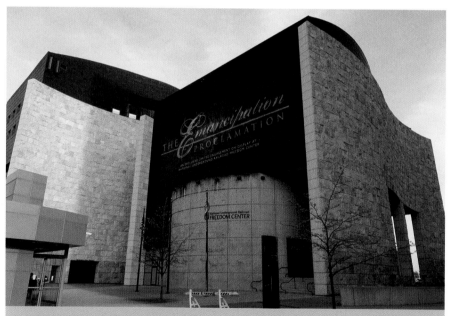

The National Underground Railroad Freedom Center is a museum in downtown Cincinnati, Ohio. Before the Civil War, Cincinnati was an important destination for runaway slaves seeking freedom in the Northern states.

SARAH GRIMKÉ, QUAKER ABOLITIONIST

The Quakers, a Christian religious sect, strongly opposed the institution of slavery, and many Quaker women played an important role in the abolitionist movement. Sarah Grimké (1792–1873) witnessed slavery firsthand as she had been born into a slave-owning family in South Carolina. From a very young age, when she saw a slave being whipped, Grimké made up her mind about the evils of slavery. As she reached adulthood, her views grew stronger. Grimké converted to the Quaker faith and became involved in the abolitionist movement as well as in working for women's equality.

In her writing, she sometimes compared the rights of women and of slaves—noting, however that slaves were far worse off. For example, she wrote, "I do not wish by any means to intimate that the condition of free women can be compared to that of slaves in suffering or degradation." In this way, she worked for the abolition of slavery and simultaneously for the full personhood of women.

Beginning in the late 1820s, Grimké and her younger sister Angelina gave public speeches and lectures, both the abolition of slavery and on women's rights. In these speeches, the sisters addressed audiences of both women and men, which was unusual for the time. They spoke about the evils of slavery and the need for it to end. Grimké also said that women should have equal opportunity, not special privileges: "All I ask of our brethren is that they will take their feet from off our necks and permit us to stand upright on the ground which God intended us to occupy."

REBECCA, CHARLEY and ROSA,
Slave Children from New Orleans.
PHOTOGRAPHED BY KIMBALL, 477 BROADWAY, N. Y.

This photograph from 1863 shows three freed slave children from New Orleans; it was circulated by abolitionists to provoke the sympathy of Northern whites. The mixed-race children were posed wearing the sort of clothes that middle class white children would wear.

slave. They traveled openly by train and steamboat from Georgia to Pennsylvania, a free state, in 1848. The pair later became speakers for the growing abolitionist movement.

Sojourner Truth is another woman who escaped slavery in 1826. Truth was born in New York about one hundred miles north of New York City. At age nine she was sold to a new owner who was reportedly quite cruel. In 1826 she managed to escape with her infant daughter, Sophia, a year before New York emancipated all slaves. Truth did remarkable things, including fighting for her son's freedom. Upon learning that her son, Peter, only five at the time, had been sold illegally, she rook the matter to court. Truth successfully challenged a white man, and won, in court. Her efforts led to the return of her son from the south. Truth later became a well-known abolitionist and speaker on the topic. She is perhaps best known for her speech, "Ain't I a Woman?" She raised questions about the connection between her race, status as a former slave, and being a woman:

> That man over there says that women need to be helped into carriages, and lifted over ditches, and to have the best place everywhere. Nobody ever helps me into carriages, or over mud-puddles, or gives me any best place! And ain't I a woman?

The daily resistances of slaves may have helped them to cope with their , but also only impacted a small number of slaves each year. Similarly, individual owners freeing their slaves was unlikely, though some slaves were granted **manumission**. The larger issue of slavery would take a much bigger act of resistance. The international slave trade legally ended in 1807, but slavery continued in the United States even after ships no longer brought new women, men, and children from Africa to be slaves. The larger abolitionist movement is closely connected with the runaway slaves, the Underground Railroad, and religious groups such as the Quakers.

Slave narratives, such as those by Harriet Jacobs, were an important data point for those working to abolish slavery. While some white abolitionists had witnessed slavery firsthand, there were countless others who had not. The stories of runaway slaves who had escaped the horrors of the institution were a powerful way to recruit more abolitionists to the cause. These narratives told of the sexual abuse of female slaves, separation of children from mothers, and extended kin, and of harsh punishments for slaves.

Women—including some who had escaped from slavery—played an important role both in the abolitionist movement. Society did not allow women many rights at this time. The women speaking out for abolition broke many of the expectations for women in society at that time. Through their stories, however, allies joined forces and fought against legal slavery.

CONCLUSION

By the time of the Civil War, there were approximately four million people living in slavery in the United States. Slavery was not limited to the American South, nor was it restricted to large plantations. Slave women worked just as hard as men, and often had even harder lives as a result. "Their bodies were owned, and their children were owned, and all were sold as commodities at the will of their owners," writes historian Wendy Warren. Marriages between slaves were ignored. Children were sold away from their mothers and fathers. Masters forced female slaves to have sex with them, and then sold both mother and baby away so as not to upset their wives.

Female slaves worked hard for their masters. They also fought back, ran away, and told their stories. Children born into slavery learned the lessons and they, too, fought back. Children sold away, ran away to reunite with their parents. Wives and husbands escaped together and made it to safety. And the abolitionists listened to their stories and fought for freedom and an end to slavery.

TEXT-DEPENDENT QUESTIONS

1. How did female slaves find ways to resist their owners on a daily basis?

2. What made Sojourner Truth's fight for the return of her son so unusual?

3. In what ways did female abolitionists challenge social norms of the time?

RESEARCH PROJECT

Read Sojourner Truth's "Ain't I A Woman?" speech (available at https://www.nps.gov/wori/learn/ historyculture/sojourner-truth.htm). What are the issues she raises in her speech? Select one of those issues and write about how it is, or is not, a current concern or issue for society today.

antebellum period—refers to the period from 1789, after the United States became an independent nation, until the Civil War began in 1861.

aristocracy—the highest class in a society.

cash crop—a crop, such as cotton or tobacco, that is produced primarily for sale at a market. Cultivation of cash crops was very labor-intensive, and required large numbers of slaves.

chattel slavery—a type of slavery in which the enslaved person becomes the personal property (chattel) of the owner and can be bought, sold, or inherited. The person is a slave for life, and their offspring are also enslaved.

domestic slave trade—the buying, selling, and transportation of enslaved people within a territory or country, such as the United States or the Spanish colonies.

Emancipation Proclamation—a presidential proclamation issued in late 1862 that declared that all African-Americans held as slaves in rebellious states during the Civil War would be considered free by the United States government on January 1, 1863.

indentured servants—a form of servitude in which a person agrees to work in exchange for food and shelter for a certain period of time.

Middle Passage—name for the slave trade route from Africa to America across the Atlantic Ocean, which was infamous due to its horrific conditions.

overseer—a plantation manager who supervised the work activities of slaves.

Quaker—a member of the Religious Society of Friends, a Christian group that was strongly opposed to slavery.

segregation—the separation of people in their daily lives based on race.

sharecropper—a tenant farmer in the South who was given credit by the landowner to pay for seeds, tools, living quarters, and food, in exchange for a share of his crop at the time of harvesting.

tenant farmer—a person who farms on rented land.

transatlantic slave trade—the capturing, enslaving, buying, selling, and transportation of Africans across the Atlantic to the Americas.

Underground Railroad—term for the route used by runaway slaves to reach freedom, either in the Northern states or Canada.

white supremacy—a belief that white people are superior to people of all other races, especially the black race, and should therefore dominate society.

slave codes—laws passed in the South to restrict the activity of slaves. Some laws made it illegal to teach slaves how to read or write. Others prevented slaves from moving freely from place to place without a pass, or from holding religious services without the presence of a white man to monitor their activities.

CHAPTER NOTES

p. 8   "In most West African societies…" Linda K. Kerber, Jane Sherron, De Hart, and Cornelia Hughes Dayton, *Women's America: Refocusing the Past*, 7th edition (New York: Oxford University Press, 2011), p. 91.

p. 10   "The law did not protect…" Kerber et al., *Women's America: Refocusing the Past*, p. 90.

p. 11   "There was snow…" William L. Andrews and Henry Louis Gates Jr., eds, *Slave Narratives* (New York: Literary Classics of the United States, 2000), p. 577.

p. 15   "Mammy, she was…" interview with Alice Green, *Born in Slavery: Slave Narratives from the Federal Writers' Project, 1936–1938*. https://www.loc.gov/collections/slave-narratives-from-the-federal-writers-project-1936-to-1938/about-this-collection/

p. 16   "cookin' for well-off white folks," ibid.

p. 18   "Women … risked scorching…" Martha B. Katz-Hyman and Kym S. Rice, eds, *World of a Slave: Encyclopedia of the Material Life of Slaves in the United States* (Santa Barbara, Calif.: Greenwood, 2011), p. 98.

p. 20   "Until mechanization…" Katz-Hyman and Rice, *World of a Slave*, p. 303.

p. 23   "The master's house…" Katz-Hyman and Rice, *World of a Slave*, p. 332.

p. 27   "Every woman had a certain…" interview with Emmaline Heard, *Born in Slavery: Slave Narratives from the Federal Writers' Project*, 1936–1938.

p. 28   "Organized into mixed-sex work gangs…" Kerber et al., *Women's America: Refocusing the Past*, p. 93.

p. 30   "Life for every young…" Katz-Hyman and Rice, *World of a Slave*, p. 540.

p. 47   "I never knowed my …" interview with Hannah Scott, *Born in Slavery: Slave Narratives from the Federal Writers' Project, 1936–1938*.

p. 48   "my White Pa," ibid.

p. 55   "I seed slaves sold..." interview with Jake Terriell, *Born in Slavery: Slave Narratives from the Federal Writers' Project, 1936–1938.*

p. 55   "My father took me away..." interview with J.W. Terrill, *Born in Slavery: Slave Narratives from the Federal Writers' Project, 1936–1938.*

p. 56   "Information wanted..." quoted in Heather Andrea Williams, "How Slavery Affected African American Families," Freedom's Story, TeacherServe©. National Humanities Center (November 16, 2018). http://nationalhumanitiescenter.org/tserve/freedom/1609-1865/essays/aafamilies.htm

p. 59   "It was a pent roof,..." Devon W. Carbado and Donald Weise, *The Long Walk to Freedom* (Boston: Beacon Press, 2012), p. 174.

p. 62   "Slave women wove resistance ..." Amrita Chakrabarti Myers, "Sisters in Arms: Slave Women's Resistance to Slavery in the United States," *Past Imperfect*, vol. 5 (1996), p. 168.

p. 62   "two instances of infanticide ..." Myers, "Sisters in Arms," p. 157.

p. 67   "That man over there..." Sojourner Truth, "Ain't I A Woman?" speech at the Women's Rights Convention in Akron, Ohio (1851). https://www.nps.gov/articles/sojourner-truth.htm

p. 68   "Their bodies were owned, and..." Wendy Warren, *New England Bound: Slavery and Colonization in Early America* (New York: Liveright Publishing, 2016), p. 12.

FURTHER READING

Anderson, Laurie Halse. *Chains*. New York: Simon and Schuster, 2011.

Andrews, William L., and Henry Louis Gates Jr. *Slave Narratives*. New York: The Library of America, 2000.

Aronson, Marc, and Marina Tamar Budhos. *Sugar Changed the World: A Story of Magic, Spice, Slavery, Freedom and Science*. Boston: Clarion Books, 2010.

Carbado, Devon W., and Donald Weise. *The Long Walk to Freedom: Runaway Slave Narratives*. Boston: Beacon Press, 2012.

Horton, James Oliver, and Lois E. Horton. *Slavery and the Making of America*. New York: Oxford University Press, 2005.

Katz-Hyman, Martha B., and Kym S. Rice, eds. *World of a Slave: Encyclopedia of the Material Life of Slaves in the United States*, Vols 1 & 2. Santa Barbara: Greenwood, 2011.

Zinn, Howard, and Rebecca Stefoff. *A Young People's History of the United States*. New York: Seven Stories Press, 2009.

INTERNET RESOURCES

https://ed.ted.com/lessons/the-courage-of-harriet-tubman-janell-hobson

This TED talk about Harriet Tubman tells of her life and work to free slaves through the Underground Railroad.

https://www.thirteen.org/wnet/slavery/experience/gender/index.html

This PBS website describes slavery, including clothes, the work, and some links to original documents to help discover our history.

https://www.loc.gov/item/mesn001/

This Library of Congress site contains the Federal Writers' Project slave narratives. In addition to the narratives, it includes photos and audio recordings.

https://www.nps.gov/hatu/index.htm

Explore the Harriet Tubman Underground Railroad National Historical Part in Maryland. This site includes information about the park and articles about Tubman's life and work.

https://www.history.com/topics/black-history/slavery

This history.com website provides background, details and photos about slavery in the United States from start until the end.

https://docsouth.unc.edu/index.html

The "North American Slave Narratives" collection at the Documenting the American South (DocSouth) web site provides introductions, summaries, and full-text of autobiographical narratives by fugitive and former slaves published in English before 1920.

1619 The first slaves arrive at the Jamestown settlement in the British colony of Virginia.

1641 Massachusetts becomes the first of the British colonies to legalize slavery. Other colonies would soon follow.

1662 The Virginia legislature passes a new law that says that children born to enslaved women are themselves slaves.

1691 Anti-miscegenation laws are passed, starting in Virginia and spreading to most states. These laws prohibit whites from marrying non-whites.

1758 Quakers vote at their yearly meeting to prohibit members from participating in slavery, either by owning slaves or by selling them.

1775 The first abolition society, the Society for the Relief of Free Negroes Unlawfully Held in Bondage, is formed in Philadelphia.

1777 Vermont becomes the first state to abolish slavery and grant full rights to all adult males.

1808 The American Slave Trade officially ends. Beyond this point all slaves are either brought to the US illegally or were born into slavery to enslaved women.

1848 The first Women's Rights Convention is held at Seneca Falls, New York. A number of prominent abolitionists speak out against slavery.

1849 Harriet Tubman escapes slavery.

1851 Sojourner Truth gives her famous "Ain't I a Woman?" speech at the Women's Rights Convention in Ohio.

1859 The last slave ship to arrive in the US lands in Alabama.

1863 Lincoln delivers the Emancipation Proclamation.

1865 Slavery officially ends with the ratification of the Thirteenth Amendment to the US Constitution.

1967 State anti-miscegenation laws are deemed unconstitutional by the US Supreme Court in the landmark case *Loving v. Virginia*.

INDEX

INDEX

AUTHOR'S BIOGRAPHY

Catherine A. Gildae, Ph.D. is a part-time senior lecturer in sociology at Northeastern University in Boston, Massachusetts. She holds a Ph.D. in Law, Policy and Society and her dissertation research examined the role of law in family life. In addition, she has two master's degrees, one in theology from Harvard Divinity School in Cambridge, Massachusetts and the other in education from Framingham State University in Framingham, Mass. Her research and teaching emphasize issues of law, work, gender, race, social class, and sexualities. She has published chapters and worked on materials related to both social problems and sexualities within the field of sociology. While Catherine continues to enjoy both teaching and writing, her primary work these days is in the Office of Institutional Effectiveness at Massachusetts Maritime Academy in Buzzards Bay, Massachusetts.

CREDITS